THE PROFITABLE PRE$$

---A PPC METHOD---

*Discover Effective Ways to Automate Processes,
Have More Control and Profit in Today's Competitive Market*

A *Goldmine* for *Printing Industry*

THE PROFITABLE PRE$$

---A PPC METHOD---

*Discover Effective Ways to Automate Processes,
Have More Control and Profit in Today's Competitive Market*

PARMESHWAR PATIDAR

Creator of PPA-Framework

Worldwide Publishing by

Pendown Press
Powered by  Gullybaba

PENDOWN PRESS
Powered by **Gullybaba Publishing House Pvt. Ltd.,**
An ISO 9001 & ISO 14001 Certified Co.,
Regd. Office: 2525/193, 1st Floor, Onkar Nagar-A, Tri Nagar,
Delhi-110035
Ph.: 09350849407, 09312235086
E-mail: info@pendownpress.com
Branch Office: 1A/2A, 20, Hari Sadan, Ansari Road,
Daryaganj, New Delhi-110002
Ph.: 011-45794768
Website: PendownPress.com

First Edition: 2022
ISBN: 978-93-5554-265-6

Layout and Cover Designed by Pendown Graphics Team
Printed and Bound in India by Thomson Press India Ltd.

DEDICATION

The Printing Industry,
The Print Community Members,
The Mumbai Mudrak Sangh,
The World Print Hub,
My Mentor Mr Sunil Rawat
My Marketing Guru Akshar Yadav
And especially my Team Indas, Who
allowed me time to finish this book.

A well-planned PPC department can change the game of your Printing plant in just ten months.

It can work wonders in your life. You can enjoy a one-month holiday with your family without interruptions of operation from the factory.

Believe me, I am talking about my experience of 18 years in the Print Industry.

The PPC department is a Goldmine that can make you more profitable and efficient.

CONTENTS

Foreword

In manufacturing industries, it's a well-known fact that it is difficult to achieve growth and work smoothly without a proper system, planning, and workflow.

It demands the implementation of PPC (Production Planning Control) in the organization, giving you the power to create, Proficiency through Commands.

I have been in the Printing Industry since 1982, and I went through several books and magazines on the Printing and packaging industries. These books and articles helped me a lot to pursue my goals. This is always necessary to keep us informed and to enhance our knowledge.

This book on PPC will guide the people in the Industry to run their establishment efficiently by saving time, minimizing wastage, inventory control, utilization of available resources, and increasing coordination among pre-press, press & post-press.

Overall, Industry people will benefit from this booklet and, hence PPC is THE GOLD MINE.

Mr. Shyamkant Jha
(PPC Expert and Print Expert)

Meet The Author

Hello, my name is Parmeshwar Patidar.

People call me "Param".

I am an entrepreneur and innovator.

A self-starter who believes that everyone should taste the adventure of starting their own business (at some point in their life – the earlier, the better).

I provide Print process automation to the Printing and Packaging Industry.

My company IndasAnalytics LLP develops, implements and supports the Print Industry in automation by the name of Indas Print ERP.

My aim in life is to become prosperous– educate people– enjoy life and do something remarkable for the Print Industry.

I am an agriculturist and organic farmer by birth and believe in providing quality food to humankind with care and respect for Mother Nature.

Who Should Read This?

Very simple, a Print business owner who wants

- A Hockey Curve Growth
- Seamless data integrations
- Smooth operations and workflow
- Sound sleep at night
- Long holidays with family

You need to trust me. After reading this book, you will find great value, and you will love me for this. I promise you 100% the value of your attention and time.

Hello, my name is Parmeshwar Patidar, your friend and community member from the World Print Hub.

I started my journey with the Print Industry 18 years ago, just after submitting my research on Speech Recognition in Hindi at the Devi Ahilya Vishva Vidhyalaya, Indore.

It was the first AI-based Speech Recognition code written for Hindi by me in the world.

At that time, I was a Robotic Engineer and, inspired by the Hollywood movie "I-Robot", was planning to build a career in humanoid robots. At that time, I got a challenge to develop a cost estimation software for the "Naidunia Printery Indore".

I took it and started writing the code with Artificial Intelligence, and this was my first experience with practical uses of software by the Industry.

It was the turning point in my life. I started a software company named Param Software Technologies (Later Param ERP Solutions India Pvt. Ltd.).

It was the time when I smelled the marvelous fragrance of the CMYK inks and saw the mesmerizing beauty of Printing science in the form of posters. I am a machine lover by nature, and I fell completely in love with the Printing machine.

After 18 years of being in love with the Printing Industry, I have worked with many Printing experts and clients. I have a significant amount of knowledge and experience in this Industry.

Today I am the Director at IndasAnalytics LLP (India's #1 Print ERP Provider) and advisory member at the World Print Hub for Print Process Automation expertise.

I love the Printing Industry due to its presence in our life from good morning to good night, and that's why I am still a scholar of Printing science.

In my 18 years of journey, I have worked with different scales of Print houses, from 1cr to 500crs turnover. And I found that magic stick, responsible for the hockey curve growth.

After closely observing the Printing Industry and its functions, I realized that the PPC department is indeed a Gold Mine for the Printing Industry.

Believe me, PPC is the Gold Mine

We need not be amazed that the PPC can do real magic in your growth and make your business as scalable as you want.

You might wonder why there is no book on PPC till now for the Print Industry even though the Print Industry is Printing books for other industries on PPC.

You would be amazed that they think that PPC will not work in the Print Industry.

But it's not true.

Just believe me, I did it, and I have worked with the top Printers who did this magic only by making a proper PPC department in their press and have grown 10X in just 7 years.

And after the perfect PPC, you will grow your business very fast in a short period.

Why this Book?

As I told you, Printing machines are my first love, and the Print Industry has given me too much.

Now it's my turn to share and give back to the Print Industry with the same passion as I get.

Due to my own success and my 18 years of long experience, people often ask me to coach and mentor them for their growth plan.

And much as I wish to, due to time constraints today, it is no longer possible for me to coach every person individually. So I have started a mission with the PPA-Framework (my new creation) to create awareness for the Printers with a passion, to make their scalable growth plan.

That's why I am sharing all my secrets, systems, knowledge and framework through this book to enable every Printing business to make a great PPC department for their unbeatable growth.

I hope the PPC making process in this book will create a radical shift in your business.

So, without wasting any further time, let's start the recipe of making the PPC Department.

PPC: The Gold Mine!

Why did I choose this title for the book? Imagine?

A Gold Mine never fails to give you gold, and a digger always gets value from it for his work.

Likewise, PPC is the only department that works for you with a golden value generation and control over the system for better productivity and profitability.

I visited more than 400+ presses and observed that the presses that have grown faster have a fantastic team in the PPC department with perfect roles and responsibility models and proper SOPs for each work.

PPC helps them be stronger and become market leaders year by year.

You can grow without a PPC to a certain level, and then you need it to go to the next step. And for further growth step by step.

"PPC is truly the Gold Mine for me; it generates profits for me without fail."

–**Abhishek Gupta**
GPH, Indore

Acknowledgements

The completion of this book could not have been possible without the participation and assistance of Mr. Vikram Kumar, my colleague who is an expert in developing the SOPs and schematics of process flow. His contribution is sincerely appreciated and gratefully acknowledged.

My mentor Akshar Yadav pushed and prompted me to share my knowledge in a book form to contribute to the Print Industry. I am very thankful to him for this motivation.

I am thankful to Mr. Shyamkant Jha for his time and attention to review this book and for giving appreciation.

CHAPTER

1

PPC is The Bahubali! The Beginning

You may not believe me, but as per Print Industry leaders and experts, PPC is a Bahubali. Like "Mahendra Bahubali" in the iconic movie.

PPC is doing and coordinating every task in the Printing press.

From coordinating the sales team to dispatch, every piece of information will be going through the PPC only, and it can handle it much better than an owner can handle everything in his mind.

The human mind has limitations for remembering things due to repetitive work and tiredness.

But the system will remain in the same state, and it will not miss anything.

So let's understand the process of making a Bahubali (PPC) in your press to win the heart of your client and rule the Mahishmati Samrajya (your Printing market).

And the important thing, is I am right here as SS Rajamouli to train your Bahubali (PPC). So, let's go ahead and do it right now.

CHAPTER

2

Why PPC?
The True Mind of the Press

Yes, it's the mind of the Printing Plant.

What does the mind do in the body?

The mind controls everything and manages every information according to its requirements and priority.

Likewise, PPC is the mind, a command center of the whole company. For each piece of information, you will rely on it.

Every department is reporting to it directly or indirectly.

As a press owner, you can get anything from the PPC and give your instructions through it to any department.

It works based on scheduling and prioritizing the jobs according to the resources and demand.

I am sure many of you would be surprised by this and wondering how it is possible. There is no need to be surprised; this is the magic of forming the right PPC structure with the roles and responsibility model and SOPs with process excellence.

Why am I so confident about this?

Because, in my journey of Indas Print ERP development, I found this key and wrote the complete sequence of code for it.

Today it is better to have a software-based system, but not necessary to begin with it. In the next chapter, I will explain how to begin it with a basic structure.

The beginning is better than nothing.

Every Printing press has some basic structure and a team in the PPC department, but they don't know the right roles and responsibilities.

Let me share an incident with you.

One day, I received a call from my existing client and friend Vipin Ji.

He said, Param Ji, I just finished a meeting with my old press friend who has a 40-year-old legacy press.

The new generation has joined the office in the last two years. But the new generation is facing challenges making a plan for the scalability of the business.

I shared your number and suggested getting in touch with you to get an ERP solution to eliminate the challenges in business growth.

I said, no issues, I will try to find the best solution for him.

In between, I got a missed call from that press owner also, and I called him back after finishing our conversation. I promised him I would visit his press.

After 2-3 days, I visited the press, and during the visit, he showed me every process defined well and managed in a structure manually.

He said that Vipin Ji had suggested starting ERP to automate the manual process digitally to get better control and data insights.

During the visit, he continuously kept demanding a demo of the ERP.

I was avoiding it because I wanted to understand the real problem first. So that I could solve it and then implement the ERP to get 100% results.

That day during the long conversation, I came to understand that:

1. He didn't have the PPC department till now.

2. Everyone was reporting him.

3. He was controlling all activities by himself.

4. Highly involved in operations and press activities.

5. Not able to focus on client meetings and marketing activities.

6. Wanted free time to plan the future expansion.

And that is why he was planning process automation through the ERP.

I advised him that the decision he had made was perfectly okay, but we needed to make the PPC department along with it.

I said, "It's simple, we should make a plan together and build the PPC department with the PPA-Framework parallel to ERP implementation, then ERP can help to get control of everything."

He said, "PPA-Framework, what is this?"

I said, "Don't worry, I will help with this part. I have created a business process automation framework, especially for the Printing and Packaging Industry."

He said, "Wow! I am very interested in understanding it and getting it implemented in my press. How can we do it?"

The Profitable Press

I said, "Let's meet next week and make a plan for it."

It was a fascinating visit, and he openly shared all the processes and issues like we all share openly with our doctor while getting treatments.

I started making a plan for next week with a clear agenda for more discovery and for planning the PPC structure. We decided to meet on Tuesday.

*For efficient, effective and economical operation in a manufacturing unit of an organization, **it is very important to have a production planning and control (PPC) system**, and we can proudly say that we have well organized PPC department to run every operation of our company systematically.*

*The book written by Mr. Parmeshwar Patidar on the PPC Department will really help Printers to understand the value of this and its benefits. **I really appreciate the work Mr. Patidar is doing in helping and educating Printers to improve their plant efficiency.***

Great work!

Dr. Deepika Singhal
Partner at Packaging India

3

Losses? Due to the Absence of PPC!

On Tuesday, I got a call from him early morning at 7.30 AM to get confirmation and pick-up me from home to discuss more while driving.

During this, he shared his life journey about how he started the press.

He said, "I started my journey from a newspaper as a marketing guy, meeting clients to get advertisements for the Sunday edition. During this, I observed the requirements of marketing collaterals at my clients, most of them were builders.

They needed posters, flyers, brochures, visiting cards, and letterheads.

At that time, only a few people had offset machines.

So it was easy to get some orders and get them Printed from a small Printer and supply them to the clients.

With this, I saw a gap, that the client was going to the Printing press and waiting for the quotation and then waiting long for his job.

It was a kick start for me to arrange some money and start Printing. I had ready clients with me and could serve them better at their doorsteps.

I started a small Printing press with a cutting machine, a two-color offset machine with just two employees in my team.

At that time, I did everything from marketing to cost estimation to invoicing. In the next six months, we started getting good orders, and I added two more people to the team to manage all the operations.

The wheel started moving, I planned to shift to a better place, with the growth of the business, new machines and processes added to the plant, team increases, clients added.

But I started to face coordination and scheduling issues with the team."

During this conversation, lots of stories popped into my mind that most press owners started their journey from a small setup like this.

It is the time when the business growth is stagnant that the owner starts to get frustrated in life.

Not able to enjoy life, very busy with the operations and activities of the plant, this causes emotional and social changes in the behavior of the person.

Sometimes it causes serious health issues.

Business is like a child, who earns money for him, so he dedicatedly puts in all efforts to make it successful.

As we reached the plant, I said to him, "I'll let you finish your work at the office. That'll give me some time to meet your people to discover their issues and skills."

After two hours of observation, I found some challenges, and we planned a meeting with the core team to get to an agreement.

So I could make a plan for them to form the PPC Department.

These are some daunting challenges that occur in the absence of PPC:

1. Most of the jobs get delayed due to verbal schedules.

2. Huge profit loss in the planning of the jobs due to deviation from estimation to production.

3. Huge inventory and dead stocks.

4. Conflicts and blame game between departments.

5. Duplicity in tools and dies.

6. Low utilization of resources causes less efficiency.

7. Sudden financial crunches due to unmanaged payment schedules.

8. Uncontrolled wastage in production.

9. Bottlenecks on the floor due to unmanaged scheduling.

10. Unplanned maintenance causes a massive loss in the plant.

11. Person dependency for every task.

12. Losing trust and credibility in the competitive market.

I was amazed that the owner agreed on all the challenges, but the team tried to cover up these challenges with the statement that it happens everywhere, we have already tried, there is no solution for it.

I said, "Don't worry, we will make a PPC department and try to improve this."

One guy who was a supervisor from the team said

PPC is the right way, but here it is not possible.

In my previous company, I was a part of it.

I tried here too, but no one is ready for it.

I said to him, "If you cooperate with us, we will do it here, and I have a plan for your plant."

"ARE YOU READY?"

I asked them in a loud and encouraging voice.

They all raised hands and shouted.

"YESSSSSS, WE NEED IT."

And magically, we started as they were all in agreement mode finally.

I asked to get some A3 sheets with pencils and erasers.

Then I gave them a Printed paper of the Mind Map to understand the activity.

4

The Mind Map–The Making of PPC

I asked them to make a mind map for it first. I gave A3 sheets to the owner to draw a mind map with inputs from the team.

Making a Mind Map is the simple and best way to visualize an idea's wireframe.

One guy asked, "Why on paper, why not on the computer?"

I said, "you can do it digitally with free tools available on the internet to draw it.

Usually, I use miro (https://miro.com/) for it, here I plotted a mind map for the basic structure of the PPC department. I showed them on my laptop.

But doing it on paper is more fruitful as our imagination works better on paper because genetically, we humans have been conditioned to express ourselves freely on paper for centuries.

Tip!

The most important thing you need to remember while doing this is that you need to do this with your core team to make it and prepare their mental state to dream about it.

Requirements for an Effective Production Planning & Control (PPC) in an organizationz:

- Appropriate organization structure with sufficient delegation of authority and responsibility at various levels of manpower.

- The right person should be deputed at the right place for the right job.

- The maximum level of standardization of inventory, tooling, manpower, job, workmanship, equipment, etc.

- Appropriate management decisions for production schedule, materials controls, inventory and manpower turnover, and product mix.

- Flexible production system to adjust any changes in demand, any problem in production or availability of materials maintenance requirements, etc.

- Estimation of accurate leads times for both manufacturing and purchase.

- The Management Information System should be reliable, efficient and supportive.

- The capacity to produce should be sufficient to meet the demand.

- The facility should be responsive enough to produce new products change of products mix and be able to change the production rates.

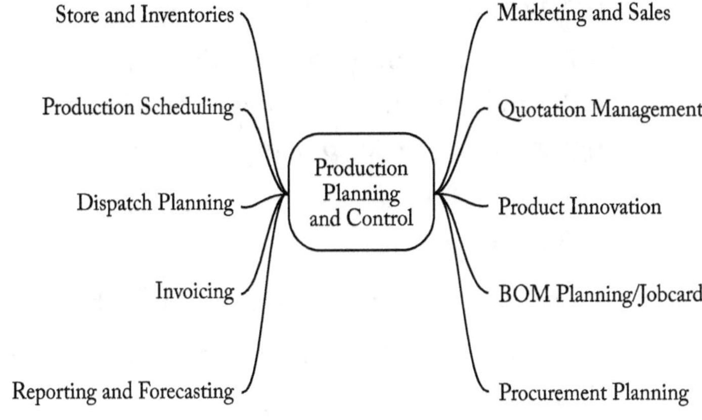

Main Objectives of Production Planning & Control (PPC):

- It is used to establish a target and check the deviations by comparing some performance measures.

- Coordinates different resources of the production system most effectively and economically.

- Coordinate among different departments.

- Elimination of bottleneck and Ensure Uninterrupted Production.

- Utilization of inventory in an optimal way.

- Smooth flow of Semi-finished material.

- Scheduling production activities to meet delivery schedule.

- Expediting the system under production.

- To ensure flexibility in the production system to accommodate changes and uncertainty.

- Optimizes the use of resources for minimum overall production cost.

- To ensure the production of the right product at the right time in the right quantity with specifications rightly suited to customers.

- Stable production system, with least confusion and undue hurry.

- Proper Coordination and Capacity Utilization.

- To produce in the right quantity and quality at the right time.

- Observing the progress of the operations and recording it properly.

- Analyzing the recorded data with the plans and measuring the deviations.

- Taking immediate corrective actions to minimize the negative impact of deviations from the plans.

- Feeding back the recorded information to the planning section to improve plans.

- Timely Delivered and reduce the lead time of the production.

Production planning and control are basically based on two different verticals. Production planning includes what to produce, when to produce, and how much to produce. Wherein, there are various control techniques in production control to ensure your Printing plant reaches optimum performance.

I have been watching Mr. Parmeshwar Patidar closely for the past two years when we started working together on our press automation. The way he is doing his hard work to make the Printers more productive is really amazing.

The book "PPC the Gold Mine" can be a game-changer for many Printing organizations that do not have a PPC department in their Printing press. I firmly believe that if you want to manage your operations in the most efficient and economical way, you must have PPC in your organization.

Mr. Sandeep Jain
Director at Manali Cartons, Chennai

CHAPTER

5

The Functions of the PPC

After having lunch together, we defined the core functions of the PPC department in the Printing Industry as the most critical part.

Apart from the standard manufacturing Industry, it is very complex to plan due to its service nature.

It was a very basic draft for the PPC as planned, but the team started to shift their viewpoint.

AMAZING!

The owner excitedly said when we wrote about the reporting of jobs that can be trackable live on the mobile with the technological implementation via ERP.

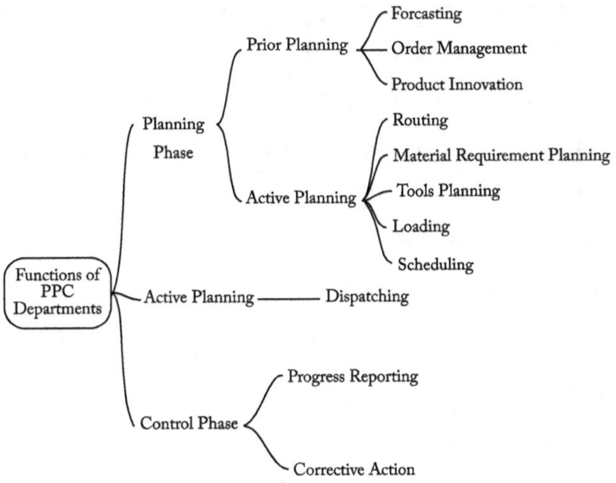

1. **Forecasting:** Estimation of quality & quantity of future work.

2. **Order management:** Giving authority to one or more persons to do a particular job.

3. **Product innovation:** Collection of specification information, bill of materials, drawing.

4. **Process planning and routing:** Find the most economical process of doing work and then decide how and where to do it?

5. **Materials planning:** It involves the determination of materials requirements.

6. **Tools planning:** It involves the requirements of tools to be used.

7. **Loading:** Assignment of work to men & m/c.

8. **Scheduling:** Planning the men and machines in the best way to get the highest productivity and efficiency. It fixes the starting and finishing time for the job.

9. **Dispatching (Execution):** It is the transition from planning to the action phase. In this phase, the team is aligned to start the actual work.

10. **Progress reporting:**

    i.   Data regarding the job progress is collected.

    ii. It is in comparison with the present level of performance.

    iii. Corrective action: Expediting the action if the progress deviates from the planning.

As we were defining functions for the PPC, the son asked me.

"Why don't we share some benefits of the PPC with the team."

I replied, "Imagine it, all issues we find in the morning, solved with the PPC department.

At the end of the day, we decided to sit the next day for the roles and responsibility model with SOPs for the PPC execution.

While returning from the factory, he offered dinner to go deeper into the transformation of the press.

There is no reason to deny the offer.

That night, I discussed with him the secret desire for this business.

I showed him the same thing after his words, on my mobile. That I had defined with so many clients during my discussions.

After dinner, I told him I had scheduled a meeting for tomorrow morning with a client. So I would reach his office directly, and the whole team should be ready for the next session after lunch.

CHAPTER

6

Benefits–Real Productive Tool

The implementation of a PPC based production system yields various advantages to any organization for various functional activities.

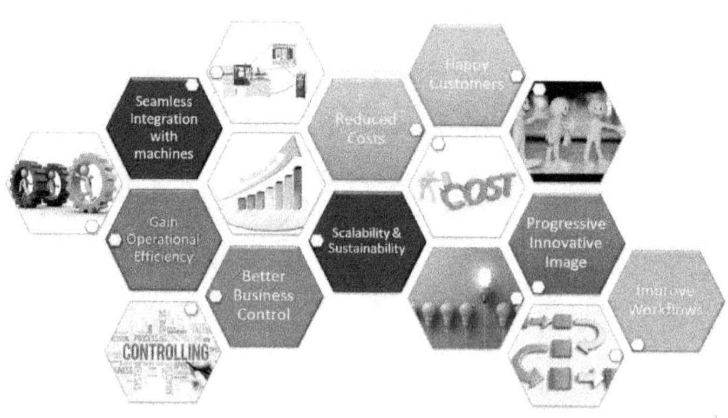

The very next day, I started with sharing a gold nugget from the PPC department.

I showed them the slide of benefits from executing the right PPC in the plant.

1. Reduces lead time and ensures timely delivery to the customers.

2. The last hour rush is avoided.

3. Problem areas of bottleneck and errors get reduced.

4. Cost reduction.

5. Optimum utilization of resources.

6. Better coordination of plant activities.

7. Benefits to workers.

8. Reduced wastage and better control over inventory.

9. Increased productivity and efficiency

10. Total control over the business

11. Higher profitability and scalability in business

12. Happy clients and employees with happy families

13. Progressive and innovative image in the competitive market

14. Hockey curve growth with the legacy model

And we started the definition of roles and responsibility models for them.

It was mind shaking activity for them.

Till now, everyone was doing everything, and now we had to define the right person for the work with the clear intent of taking responsibility.

We designed these with the RACI model for basic understanding.

CHAPTER

7

RACI–Roles And Responsibility Model

RACI is a basic model for roles and responsibilities in the modern era to handle the PPC tasks by the team in the right way.

RACI stands for responsible, accountable, consultation, and informed. The way how each of the four components is defined:

1. **Responsible:** a manager or team member who is directly responsible for completing a project task.

2. **Accountable:** the person with final authority over the successful completion of the specific task or deliverable.

3. **Consulted:** someone with unique insights the team will consult.

4. **Informed:** a client or executive who isn't directly involved, but you should keep up to speed.

Sample Sheet

Roles	Ashok	Manish	Rakesh	Mahesh
Cost Estimation	Responsible	Consulted	Informed	Accountable
Sales Order	Accountable	Informed	Responsible	Informed
Job card Creation	Consulted	Responsible	Consulted	Accountable
Inventory Planning	Informed	Accountable	Informed	Consulted

Roles & Responsibilities of the PPC:

- Forecasting the demands of the customers for the products and services.

- Prepare the production budget in advance (if possible).

- Design the facility layout.

- Specify the types of machines, equipment, and plant capacity.

- Appropriate production requirements of the raw materials, labour, and machinery.

- Prepare the necessary documents, i.e., product master, job card, material requisitions, etc.

- Drawing the schedule of the production and dispatch plans considering the maintenance schedule.

- Confirming the shortage or any excess of the end product.

- Coordination with different departments and getting the correct information to avoid gaps.

- Plans are drawn for any sudden surge in the demand for the product.

PPC Should also be aware of the following:

- Seasonal Variations

- Test Marketing

- After Sales Service

- Losses due to Unpredictable Factors

- Losses due to Predictable Factors

During the conversation on the definition of roles and responsibilities I observed lots of conflicts getting resolved.

The team seemed more confident about the new alignment of work.

"Sequence"

This was the new insight about the PPC department they found in this entire activity. The sequence is essential in every activity, whether you make movies or do business.

A new team member asked, "Sir! I have a question?

How to do the job in the right way? Is there any structure for it?"

"Yes! Yes! We have the next session on this only after the tea break".

CHAPTER

8

Sop–Process Excellence

After the tea break, I opened my magic box, my laptop.

And I asked some questions in the general discussion.

"Is the Print Industry a Manufacturing Industry?"

I got a mixed answer, both yes and no.

I asked again.

"Is the Print Industry a Service Industry?"

Again, they gave mixed answers.

I said, "The Printing Industry is a super blend of manufacturing and service both."

So, we need different SOPs for its PPC department.

Then someone asked, "What do you mean by SOP, Sir?

I said,

"SOP means Standard Operating Procedure!"

I continued,

"Standard Operating Procedure is the best example of process excellence, and you know the Printing Industry is a super blend of the manufacturing and service sector.

Have a look at what sequence we should follow:"

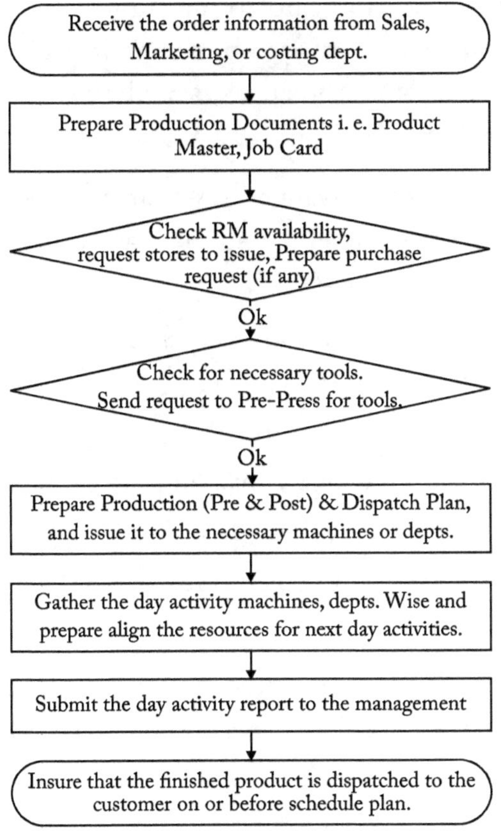

So, there is no final version of SOP that will be perfect. Every SOP will be at the pace of evolution with time. Whenever you feel you need improvements in it, make changes and test it.

After continuous improvements in Indas Print ERP as a great PPC tool, we even learned from our users to improve it.

We revised our Job card format more than 15 times till now, and people are surprised by seeing it and telling us this is the best, but as a scholar, we say always, this is final till the next version only.

In simple words, I want to say that we need not wait for perfection to start implementation. Start with a very simple SOP.

"So, we are going to make our SOPs here?" he asked.

I said, "NO........!

Making SOPs for the PPC department is a long process that requires a one-to-one consultation and dedicated time.

I am giving you some formats for it. Just follow them first, then during the implementation of ERP, we will improve again.

I have even started an activity to fulfill this gap by a free online master class twice a month. To help the people who want to make these SOPs for their PPC departments. After this, you can plan a personal discussion with my team to help build it perfectly."

As I shared the SOPs, they asked me

"How to use these SOPs?"

I said, get Printouts and give them to the respective person to paste on his desk and ask him to follow the sequence.

The next day after defining everything, they asked for the demo of the Indas Print ERP.

It took about one month for the whole process of refining the PPC activities and implementing the ERP.

Let me conclude.

9

Bahubali 2.0–The Conclusion

Let's come to the conclusion of the story again with Bahubali 2.0,

For both Bahubali and PPC, the conclusion is the same.

After removing all hurdles from Mahishmati Samarjya, Bahubali ruled successfully for many years.

And so is the case with PPC. After removing all hurdles from your Printing business, PPC will help you rule the market forever.

How can I know and claim this?

Interesting!

I can make this claim about Bahubali because I am a Historian by nature & interest and found the real Mahishmati Samarajya. It was not in the south. It is Maheshwar today at the bank of the Narmada River in Madhya Pradesh.

Whatever SS Rajamouli picturized in the movie, most of those things are available in the history of the Omkareshwar and Avantika Kingdoms.

I observed closely in the movie that the Shiva Lingam, river, castle, ghats, waterfall, bulls, and the associated states everything touches history. Like me, if you find it interesting, you can google it and explore this further.

But coming back to the context of this book, for PPC, I can make this claim because I have worked on it, developed it and used it successfully in the Print Industry.

Okay, so the bottom line is that after making the right PPC department with perfect roles and responsibilities, you can rule like Bahubali in the competitive market, as a big Samarajya.

Because now you have a strong army of people with the perfect work culture in the PPC department. The central command center for every decision and action.

CHAPTER

10

The Next Steps– What to do?

Very simple, you have two choices.

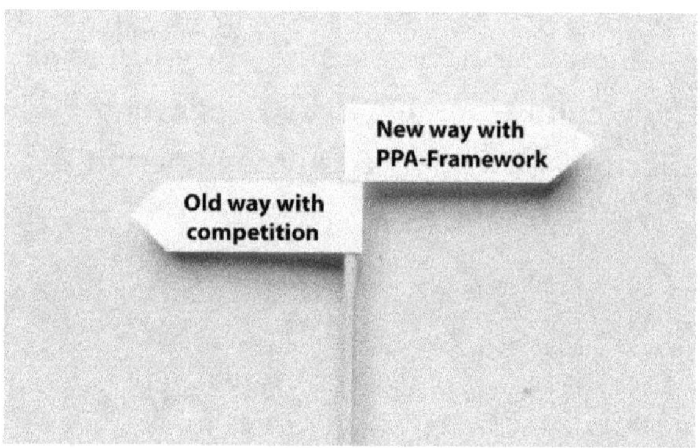

Continue with the old system and improve as required with learnings. You will reach the desired goal one day.

It may take a long time with the market competition and all the challenges you are facing today.

The Profitable Press

Or

Be distinct in the market to rule it, implement the PPA-Framework, form a perfect PPC department, and innovate to lead the market and get the Hockey Curve Growth in a year.

The new way will open the doors to:

- Finish the competition.
- Be a sustainable and scalable business.
- Be the market leader.

The choice is yours; you can add me to your tribe to make your PPC structure and plan the growth roadmap.

Free Tool Kit
To Start Your PPC

Thank you for taking the first step to orienting your Print Operations toward profitability. This toolkit is my gift to you for moving in the right direction. This toolkit covers adoptive SOPs and charts to fix your PPC Department.

Download all resources to use them in the growth plan of your business.

Please visit the link to download:

https://www.ppa-framework.com/ppc-thegoldmine

Or scan the QR code